The Dark Side of the Vietnam Conflict:

Individual Deviance or Organizational Evil

Manfred F. Meine and Thomas P. Dunn

PROLOGUE

While some may argue that once again examining events that

occurred during the Vietnam conflict seems rather dated at this

point, there continue to be issues worth discussing, if for no other

reason than for the lessons they may provide for the present. With

frequent publication of books and television documentaries about

that war, highlighting not only the call to duty and the sacrifices of

those who served in Vietnam, but also the emotional pain they

experienced directly as a result of the pressures and horrors of the

conflict, but also because of their treatment at home, continuing

examination of the Vietnam experience seems quite appropriate. It

can even be argued that the country's current focus on supporting its

military engaged in the seemingly never ending conflicts in the

Middle East, may have its roots in a "national guilty conscience"

about the treatment of Vietnam Era veterans at the time of that

1

Side of the Vietnam Conflict

conflict. In order to categorize and better understand the individual

and organizational behaviors discussed in this work, the authors

turned to the seminal treatise on crime and deviance in the military,

Khaki Collar Crime: Deviant Behavior in the Military Context, by

Dr. Cliff Bryant, who combined his first-hand observations as a

military police officer with his unrelenting enthusiasm for innovative

scholarship and academic excellence. In keeping with that tradition,

this book 1) incorporates the firsthand experiences of its first author,

as supported by a number of books and writings dealing with "dark

side" events during America's Vietnam experience and 2) employs

Bryant's conceptual framework of Intra-occupational Crime which

he defines as crimes against persons, property and performance

internal to the military setting; Extra-occupational Crime which he

defines as crimes against persons, property and performance

external to the military setting both in the American civilian social

setting and in foreign social settings and finally, Inter-occupational

Crime which he defines as crime in relation to the enemy military

with the inherent utilization of his innovative concept of Crimes

Against Performance. Bryant's concepts and definitions are

considered in conjunction with Jurkiewicz and Grossman's

insightful delineation of "organizational evil" to suggest that 1) war

does indeed result in seemingly good people doing evil things, but

also to suggest that 2) beyond the unfortunate, but inevitable,

idiosyncratic evil, political and organizational factors may also lead

to organizations engaging in evil practices. Such evil may be the

result of policies or actions which can lead to 1) organizations taking

little or no action when unethical behaviors emerge, or 2) the tacit

acceptance of unethical actions, i.e., "looking the other way," and, in

extreme situations, even 3) the overt routinization of systemic

unethical behaviors within the organization. As such, these events

could very well have served to perpetuate public perceptions of "evil

organizations" in general, and the military in particular, as opposed

to the embarrassing, but, arguably, less inflammatory occurrences of

individual deviance within an organization. While at first glance

there may be little difference in the outcome and in the type of

behavior, it is the organizational setting which may provide an

environment that fosters or permits deviance that is the key to

understanding events such as those that took place during the

Side of the Vietnam Conflict

Vietnam War, and are likely to occur in any war. Bryant even

suggests that, "In the final analysis, certain kinds of deviant behavior

on the part of military personnel, and conditions and circumstances

that foster deviancy, actually are latently functional to the mission of

the military and, as such, are tacitly, if not actively endured and even

promoted" (Bryant, 1979, p.67).

INTRODUCTION

Although the Vietnam War may well be just an unsettling memory

for many Americans, it remains a perpetual topic of both pragmatic

interest and scholarly inquiry, and in addition to books continuing to

be published about that conflict, it is not uncommon to find

television documentaries about the American experience in Vietnam,

or to see video collections for sale in stores.

Based in large part on the first-hand observations of the first

author, while serving as a supervisory Special Agent in the Army's

Criminal Investigation Division, and utilizing a conceptual

framework that combines the more general concept of organizational

evil, defined by Jurkiewicz and Grossman as "the institutionalization

of a set of principles whose purpose is to knowingly harm

individuals..." (2012, p3), with Bryant's (1979) more specific

typological approach, this book re-visits one of the most socio-

economically volatile periods in American history, with a view

toward illuminating and analyzing some of the lesser known

examples of military crime and deviance that occurred during the

Vietnam War.

If, however, the Vietnam War is indeed but a memory, why

would a discussion of events during that war be of interest today?

The answer may well lie in the continuing focus on the conflict, both

in frequent comparisons to more recent wars, and the occasional

examination of alleged "evils" reportedly perpetrated by US Forces

in Vietnam, one of the more recent being the quite startling but

extensively documented chronicle of such so-called war crimes, *Kill

Anything that Moves* (Turse, 2013). The furor raised and the

apology successfully demanded of CBS Television for using the

Side of the Vietnam Conflict

memorial wreckage of a B52 Bomber in Hanoi, Vietnam as the

backdrop for a reality show also attests to the continuing emotional

importance of the Vietnam War (Hinkley, *New York Post*, March 24,

2013).   That continuing interest and a contentious and emotional

panel discussion of the book *The Foundations of Organizational Evil*

(2012) at the 2012 American Society for Public Administration

Annual Conference, about this article, led to this further examination

of the phenomenon of organizational evil and any potential

relationship between organizations and events related to the Vietnam

Conflict supported by the second author's career-long interest in the

work and legacy of Dr. Cliff Bryant.

CONCEPTUAL FRAMEWORK

Organizational Evil

 While the evil behavior of human beings could conceivably reflect

only the actions of individual actors, the fact that even the most

complex of social organizations are, in essence, just a collectivity of

individuals as noted by Jurkiewicz and Grossman (2012, p. 3-4) and,

as such, the behaviors of a collection of individuals can persist in moving to the extreme, with the resulting evil being so pervasive as

to warrant its being meaningfully conceptualized as organizational

evil, *per se.* More specifically, beyond the unfortunate, but

inevitable instances of idiosyncratic evil, it seems clear that political

agendas and socio-economic factors may also contribute

significantly to the phenomenon of organizational evil; with such

evil being manifested in 1) organizations taking little or no action

when unethical behaviors emerge, 2) the tacit acceptance of

unethical actions, i.e., "looking the other way," and, in extreme

situations, even 3) the overt routinization of systemic unethical

behaviors within the organization . As such, these events could well

have and may continue to perpetuate and lend legitimacy to the

public perceptions of "evil organizations" as opposed to the

embarrassing, but, arguably, less inflammatory occurrences of

seemingly good people doing evil things within an organization. It

should be noted that although Bryant's typological approach

constitutes his primary contribution to this commentary, his

observations regarding the latent functionality of deviance in the

accomplishment of military missions, are clearly commensurate with

Side of the Vietnam Conflict

Jurkiewicz and Grossman's conceptualization and treatment of

organizational evil.

The Bryant Typology

In his seminal treatise on crime and deviance in the military, *Khaki*

Collar Crime: Deviant Behavior in the Military Context, Bryant

(1979) combined his first-hand observations as a military police

officer with his unrelenting enthusiasm for innovative and

provocative scholarship and academic excellence. Specific examples

reflecting Vietnam's dark side will be discussed within the

framework of Bryant's categorization of criminal behavior in the

military; namely, Intra-occupational Crime: crimes against persons,

property and performance internal to the military setting, Extra-

occupational Crime: crimes against persons, property and

performance external to the military setting both in the American

civilian social setting and in foreign social settings and Inter-

occupational Crime: crime in relation to the enemy military, with the

inherent utilization of his innovative concept of Crimes Against

Performance.

Utilizing the dual conceptual framework described above, an
examination of selected events occurring during the Vietnam
Conflict will be used to suggest insights worthy of inclusion in the
seemingly timeless debate regarding the efficacy of the concept of
organizational evil   vis-à-vis the evil behavior of individuals within
an organizational context. The fact that some of the war's most
disturbing organizational evils or grossly unethical individual
behaviors have only recently come to light makes such a discussion
one of contemporary interest.

AMERICA'S LOST WAR: A BRIEF HISTORICAL PERSPECTIVE

Without question this country can be justifiably proud of its
contemporary military. Despite years of an incessant and demanding
operational tempo, long wars, and repeated deployments, today's US
military is arguably a professional force unlike any before (The
Evolution of the All-Volunteer Force, 2006). Regardless of the
frequently touted national pride in the professionalism and the
resultant public support of America's military forces, a support that

Side of the Vietnam Conflict

was certainly lacking during the Vietnam Conflict (Powell, 2012; Westheider, 2007), more recent events, such as the alleged prisoner torture at Abu Ghraib in Iraq and, arguably, some unacceptable actions in Afghanistan (Hersh, 2004) have again demonstrated that war does result in unfortunate events and behaviors even among otherwise "good" people that ideally should have been prevented. Unfortunately, no matter how undesirable such recent behaviors may be, they appear to pale in comparison to a number of events noted in this commentary or those detailed by Turse (2013) that reportedly occurred during the Vietnam War.

The phenomenon of war leading to unwanted events and individually deviant behaviors was certainly present during the Vietnam Conflict. Regrettably, problems during that conflict were exacerbated by social problems at home, the widespread lack of public support for the war and the military, leadership problems, a partially conscripted force, and other social, political and policy related issues (Powell, 2012; Sitikoff, 1999). This commentary focuses on these and other problems encountered in Vietnam as a way to examine the phenomenon that during war, good people may well resort to doing bad things, possibly in political and organizational environments, making such behaviors more likely. The discussion further suggests that while much positive change may have indeed taken place over the years, it is important to remain vigilant lest mistakes of the past be repeated. Hyperbole aside, it seems imperative to acknowledge that inappropriate behaviors, both individually and collectively, in military forces occur on all sides of a conflict, and there was no shortage of such violations, even atrocities, by Vietcong and North Vietnamese forces such as the Massacre at Hue (Anonymous, 1969; Rummel, 1997).

The Vietnam War was, by any standard, unique in the annals of American History, especially since it was the first war to have been branded as a war the United States lost (Nelan, Angello and Thompson, 1995; Sitikoff, 1999). While it was arguably not lost on the battlefield, the scenes of people being plucked from the roof of the US Embassy in Saigon as North Vietnamese troops took control of the city, with the same evacuation helicopters subsequently being unceremoniously dumped from the decks of aircraft carriers into the sea, the conclusion, still so painfully frustrating for countless

Americans, that the war was indeed lost, at least politically, cannot be credibly denied (Jenkins, 2005). Despite the so-called loss, it is important to not overlook the sacrifices of the nation's military and supporting civilians in that war, as evidenced by the more than 58,000 names on the Vietnam Memorial wall in Washington DC (The Wall, 2012). Another unique aspect of that war is that it was the first war played out in America's living rooms. Films of events were rushed out of country to be shown in daily newscasts, with the one or two day delay forced by the fact that the internet and other modern technologies were not yet available, not to mention the fact that contemporary military actions are frequently made available to the American public in real time.

Concurrently, it is clear that all was not well with a military that had been called upon to fight a logistically difficult and increasingly unpopular war, a war that led to many organizational problems for the military to include numerous incidents of deviant behavior and crime in the military setting. Unlike today's military conflicts, Vietnam was America's last war that relied to a great degree on a conscripted force. Unfortunately the conscription process led to significant fairness issues, with deferments frequently

being granted to those who were married or enrolled in college

(Card, 2000). In retrospect, it would seem to have been inevitable

that the institution and application of deferments alone during the

Vietnam Era would generate a resounding chorus of volatile

accusations that the potentially life threatening conscription process

had been systematically designed to favor draft-eligible young men

from among the higher socioeconomic statuses (Westheider, 2007).

The large number of deferments may also have contributed to

a shortage of conscripts. This possible shortage was addressed in

part by what has been termed "McNamara's 100 thousand." That

initiative allowed people not normally eligible for military service or

the draft because of limited physical and mental qualifications to be

enlisted despite their shortcomings. The program was touted as an

effort to allow more of the less privileged to take advantage of the

benefits of military service—which, of course, added to the

perception that those very people the program claimed to help, bore

a disproportionate brunt of the war (Westheiser, 2007; Greenhill,

2006; Greenberg, 1969).

The military during the Vietnam Era, not unlike today, was a reflection of American society, and the war took place during many of the years so well known for the civil rights struggle. The racial strife occurring at home also took place in the military—with troops in uniform openly participating in racial demonstrations both in Vietnam and in other foreign areas (Author Note 1). In addition to racial tension, the military in Vietnam and elsewhere also suffered from the growing drug culture in America. Once again, the same problem ballooned in the military, with drug use rampant in Vietnam, an abuse that consumed most of the military's law enforcement resources (2). In addition to the overt ramifications of these two problems individually, when taken together, their less obvious impact may well have included a contribution to what became a particularly debilitating problem for the military in Vietnam; namely, that of inexperienced leadership within the company grade officer corps. (Westheider, 2007).

BRYANT'S "KHAKI COLLAR" LEGACY

As the previously mentioned and widely publicized contemporary events in the Iraq and Afghanistan conflicts have shown, war not only leads to very noble and heroic actions on the part of fighting

forces, but can also lead to disturbing incidents of crime and

delinquency. Unfortunately, Vietnam was no exception. The

following examination of illustrative "dark side" events during the

Vietnam War via Bryant's typology is submitted with an

acknowledgement that, not unlike most qualitative social science

typologies, the categories may be less than definitively distinct.

- Intra-occupational Crime: crimes against persons, property
  and performance internal to the military setting such as the
  military club scandal chronicled in the book *The Khaki Mafia*
  and the numerous, and still unsettling , incidents of
  "fragging."

Long before the Vietnam Era, recreational clubs had been

established on military instillations to provide entertainment for

troops, especially those deployed overseas. Of particular interest

was the fact that these overseas clubs permitted gambling in the form

of slot machines. As one might expect, slot machines, especially in

enlisted and non-commissioned officer clubs were a lucrative

enterprise, with the huge profits enabling the clubs to offer lavish

entertainment. Of course big money leads to big temptation, and in

the early 60's a clique of clearly self-interested deviant club managers, all senior non-commissioned officers, developed in Augsburg, Germany then home of the Army's 24th Infantry Division. This clique became quite adept at skimming profits and improperly awarding winnings to officials they needed to influence. When a key member of the clique moved to Fort Bragg, NC the entire clique was transferred there, followed by the group going to Vietnam where they continued their activities (Moore & Collins, 1971).

This situation was brought to light by a courageous officer and was fully investigated, but the investigation was initially "squashed." The case was later reopened and led to Congressional hearings, the results of which included the professional downfall of at least one general and the first sergeant major of the Army. Although these high-profile events inevitably resulted in the prohibition of gambling in military clubs, it would seem, in retrospect, similarly inevitable that vested political interests would be successful in blocking any attempt to enact criminal prosecutions, and none were forthcoming (Moore & Collins, 1971; {6}).

Of course Vietnam also saw its share of property diversion and theft since thousands of tons of material came into the country, often without adequate accountability. It was a routine topic of conversation among troops in Vietnam that if someone needed a vehicle part or uniform item, it was often easier to utilize the Blackmarket downtown than to obtain it through official channels.

While the previous examples of Intra-occupational crime are significant, there can be no doubt that the most severe and insidious example of crime internal to the military structure were the frequent, and still disconcerting instances of "fraggings," within the ranks, with several hundred officers and NCO's being killed by their own troops, and countless others being injured. (Brush, 2010; Westheider, 2007; {7}).

Two of the particularly interesting, and because of their positive ending a bit more palatable, fragging situations are ones which may well describe the luckiest men alive. In both cases soldiers attempted to kill their leaders. In the first a disgruntled soldier ordered to perform guard duty turned his loaded rifle toward his senior non-commissioned officer and pulled the trigger. Although the weapon functioned normally and the firing pin struck the primer, the bullet did not go off. Fortunately, the soldier was subdued before he could try again. In the second case, a soldier

placed a hand grenade with the spoon taped closed, and after pulling

the safety pin placed it into the gas tank of his commander's Jeep.

While the tape dissolved as planned, and the pin functioned

normally, the grenade did not explode. In both of these instances,

laboratory examination did not disclose why these munitions did not

fire—hence they may well have been the "luckiest men alive" at the

time (8). Unfortunately for others, disgruntled soldiers were often

more successful in these "fraggings."

- Extra-occupational Crime: crimes against persons, property
  and performance external the military setting both in the
  American civil social setting and in foreign social settings
  such as profiteering and blackmarketing which led to the
  underreported deserter village in the Cholon District of
  Saigon and the fascinating exploits of an ingenious Special
  Forces Captain.

While some undesirable actions and behaviors were directly

related to the war effort, as in every war, self-centered profiteering

also took place during the Vietnam conflict. Arguably, the pressures

of the war, leadership failings, the drug problem, and other problems

led to a significant number of soldiers becoming deserters in

Vietnam, thus providing a particularly illustrative example of behaviors that are categorized by Bryant as Crimes against

Performance. Many of these deserters ended up in the Cholon

District of Saigon in what was loosely referred to as the deserter

village, a place so dangerous even military police were wary of entry

without significant force. It was here that many of the deserters

engaged in Extra-occupational Blackmarket activities (Cholon,

2012) or were recruited by the Vietnamese underworld to travel

throughout South Vietnam with false documents allowing them to

use "military payment certificates or scrip" to purchase green dollars

or dollar instruments which were highly sought after by well to do

Vietnamese and Chinese merchants for export to off shore banks,

including banks in the US (4).

Although unrelated to a deserter situation, another interesting

case of what may arguably be termed either Extra-occupational

crime or Inter-occupational crime, although not related to a deserter

situation, was a Special Forces Captain who was found to have

converted over $250,000 and who had purchased seven Corvette

Automobiles in the US, all picked up by people using his name at

various dealerships in the US. The source of the funds was reported to have been a cache of dollars found during a Special Forces

operation—a find that was not reported (5).

- Inter-occupational Crime: Crime in relation to the enemy
  military such as the execution of an enemy double agent
  chronicled in the book *Murder in War Time and the* Mỹ Lai
  massacres as well as those described in the book *The Tiger
  Force*.

A rather intriguing and unique Inter-occupational event was the

"cloak and dagger" operation in which US Special Forces soldiers

executed a suspected Vietnamese double agent despite being warned

not to by the CIA. The execution took place on a boat in Nha Trang

Bay, with the body being thrown overboard. When a member of the

execution team communicated his "cold feet" to his co-conspirators,

he felt threatened by his compatriots and went to military law

enforcement officials. The ensuing investigation and attempted

cover-up led to the Commander of Special Forces in Vietnam being

placed in pre-trial confinement—the highest ranking person ever to

be so confined. As a team of Army investigator's was on route to

arrest the Special Forces legal counsel, the investigation was

inexplicably terminated. In the end, no one was prosecuted for this

murder (*Murder in War Time,* Stein, 1992; {3}).

Side of the Vietnam Conflict

Without doubt, the most publicized Inter-occupational war crime event in Vietnam was the Mỹ Lai massacre during which a large number of unarmed Vietnamese villagers were killed by a platoon of the Americal Division (Raimondo, undated). If it were not for the selfless intervention of some helicopter crews, the toll might have been even higher. Lieutenant Calley, the young platoon leader, was the only person successfully prosecuted for the event, and although initially sentenced to life in prison, he only served a few years under house arrest (Allen, 2006). While Mỹ Lai may not have been the most serious of such unfortunate events, it could certainly be argued that it was Mỹ Lai that disproportionally demonstrated the need for more and better volunteers to provide leadership for the troops since the number of well-trained and experienced career soldiers on the front lines dropped sharply as casualties and combat rotation took their toll, the latter because of the one-year tours and individual replacement policies for troops assigned to Vietnam (Kaplan 1987 and Westheider, 2007).

What may well have been the most serious and systematic series of Inter-occupational war crimes, arguably of the type Bryant suggests may have tacit organizational approval, has been chronicled in the book *The Tiger Force*. The Tiger Force was a Long Range Reconnaissance platoon of the 101st Airborne Division which used the establishment of "free fire zones" to justify indiscriminately killing numerous unarmed civilians, resulting in part from the widespread "body count," mentality that was used to measure the success of operations in Vietnam (Gartner and Myers, 1995). Those killings would never have come to light if the former head of Army Criminal Investigation had not copied investigative reports which he secreted upon retirement, while arranging for them to be made available upon his death. The investigative files relating to those events finally became public just a few years ago upon that death and they resulted in the cited book. While these events were investigated during the Vietnam Conflict, Washington politics at the highest levels stopped the investigation in the aftermath of the Mỹ Lai scandals. Once again, no prosecutions resulted (Sallah and Weiss, 2006). Unfortunately, Turse's more recent book, while also mentioning the Tiger Force's operations, suggests that such actions were not isolated occurrences (2013).

To this point, the discussion has highlighted the fact that military conflicts result in some people doing bad things in the name of war and while some of the events were a direct part of the war, others were just an exploitation of opportunities for some quick personal profit. Regardless of the reason behind these behaviors, it has been suggested that questions relating to the quality of organizational leadership in Vietnam may well have been contributing factors to the level of deviance encountered during that war.

PROACTIVE LEADERSHIP: PART OF THE PROBLEM OR THE SOLUTION?

"An excellent organization with poor leadership won't work; an imperfect organization with good leadership will." (Rumsfeld, 2011)

While the primary focus of this commentary has been to illuminate some of the more regrettable incidents of deviant behavior that occurred during the Vietnam War, some insights not only into how they might have been avoided, but, more importantly, how the relevant lessons learned in Vietnam might serve to reduce similarly disturbing incidents in contemporary (e.g., Iraq and Afghanistan) as well as future, military assignments, would appear to be not only appropriate, but unavoidable.

Although human social behavior in general , and military behavior in Vietnam in particular , is much too complicated to be explained in terms of any single cause, the centrality of proactive leadership in promoting and enforcing ethical behavior within complex organizations has been recognized as one of the most crucial aspects in reducing unethical behavior (Meine and Dunn, 2012). Unfortunately, leadership, while legitimately touted as a solution, may well have been a significant part of the problem in Vietnam. If that assertion is accurate, it is appropriate to examine the leadership challenges that surfaced during the Vietnam War.

This commentary is not intended to paint a comprehensively negative picture of the American military, since most of the troops who served their country in Vietnam arguably performed their duties as prescribed, with many having done so with documented distinction, and at great personal and sometimes ultimate sacrifice.

And yet, it is clear that there were significant deviance problems in Vietnam. Although the categories in Bryant's typology are useful in the ongoing efforts to further comprehend the nature of deviant behavior and crime in the military setting, they do not, in and of themselves, contribute to an understanding of why the Vietnam conflict was one during which an arguably larger number of such behaviors than might have been anticipated took place.

While admittedly disconcerting, accusations of a breakdown of leadership in Vietnam have not been uncommon. If such accusations are warranted, they could be explained in part by the previously noted Intra-occupational deviant behaviors involving the problem of drug abuse as well as racial strife and tensions, but there are likely also some organizational causes. The existence of the draft and McNamara's 100K may have had an influence on the leadership question, as did the need for replacement officers and Non Commissioned Officers (NCO's) creating shortages of highly qualified personnel. Those factors led to Army officers becoming Captains (the typical rank of company commanders) with only two years of service. As a result, company commanders were 1) frequently lacking in military experience and 2) often in possession of less formal education than their predecessors; since, during the Vietnam Era, the requirement for possessing a college degree as a prerequisite for becoming a commissioned office was frequently waived. To aggravate the situation, commanders were often taken out of command positions after only six months to allow more officers to gain combat command experience. Unfortunately that meant they left their positions about the time they began to be most comfortable with the demanding responsibilities of combat command. Inexperienced leaders may have also contributed to the development of what "Time Magazine" called "the mere gook rule." A phenomenon, that resulted in little or no punishment when the victim of a violent crime, even murder was Vietnamese rather than a fellow American (Allen, 2006).

Leadership issues at all levels may also have contributed to broader military problems inherent in the Vietnam War resulting in a military that has been termed the "hollow force"—that is, a force significantly depleted in morale, capabilities and equipment (Chief of Staff of the Air Force Strategic Studies Group, 2011).

SUMMARY and CONCLUSIONS

In keeping with its primary focus, this commentary has sought to illuminate, via the first-hand experiences of the first author, combined with additionally relevant evidence from books and other writings, some of the "dark side" events that occurred during the Vietnam conflict. While some of the events, such as the My Lai massacre, were highly publicized, others (e.g., the military clubs scandal and the deserter village in the Cholon District in Saigon) were not subjected to similarly intense public scrutiny and are not as well known. In the process, some significant ancillary issues, such as the lack of public support for the war, drug abuse and racial issues, and the influence of innovative television coverage, were introduced and judged to have had a major contextual influence on the deviant behavior and crime that were the article's central concern. Conceptually, Bryant's innovative typology and Jurkiewicz and Grossman's insightful delineation of "organizational evil" provided the overall framework for the analysis. While it is important to acknowledge that evidence derived from even the most prevalent and pertinent anecdotes does not constitute empirical verification, such illustrative material can, when appropriately documented, provide meaningful support for conclusions derived from qualitative analyses.

First, the unavoidable answer to the question raised in the title of this commentary can only be a resounding yes! Yes to incidents of seemingly "good" people committing evil behaviors individually within the military context *and* yes to the existence of organizational evil in keeping with Jurkiewicz and Grossman's definition of the phenomenon.

Deviant behaviors committed by individual combatants representing both sides of a military conflict are likely inevitable in any war; and, as demonstrated herein, such was certainly the case with a number of American military organizations and individual troops in Vietnam. The basic fact that troops are trained to overcome an enemy through lethal military force, and are ceremoniously rewarded for successfully doing so, requires a strong emphasis on proper values to avoid a "slippery slope" of evil that can evolve into not only the demonization of the enemy's military combatants, but, as evidenced in part by the "mere gook rule" appears to have been the case in Vietnam, with an entire population becoming similarly demonized (James, 2003).

While the discussion of fraggings and deserters becoming involved in criminal activities may provide little, if any, support for positing the existence of organizational evil within the American military, events such as those described in the books *Murder in War time, Tiger Force, Kill Anything that Moves* and *The Khaki Mafia* clearly suggest that such occurrences resulted from an organizational subculture that included a favorable environment for the viability of these and perhaps similar activities. As such, these events could reasonably be interpreted as indications of the existence of the previously defined evil at an organizational level. In addition, since so much of the military and political focus during the Vietnam War was on "body count" as a measure of success for military units and of perhaps paramount importance, their leaders (Sullivan, 2005; Gartner & Myers, 1995), an argument that the stage had been irreparably set for the evolvement of organizational evil might be very difficult to refute.

Secondly, the analysis of selected dark side Vietnam War events also generated some unanticipated, but nonetheless important conclusions, with regard to future initiatives in the area of further establishing and maintaining an ethical military force. The primary conclusion is arguably that strong and effective ethical leadership may well be critical in the prevention of both individual evil and organizational evil (Meine and Dunn). Perhaps of equal importance were the detrimental ramifications of the lack of public support for the military during the Vietnam Conflict. While specific conclusions based on limited examples may not be justified it does seem reasonable to ask if the treatment of military personnel during that war, and the lack of public support for the war itself, served to exacerbate the unique problems that were unavoidably inherent in the conduct of a war in Southeast Asia. If that is the case, then what may arguably be one of the most important lessons of events during the Vietnam War is that political and military leaders need to focus on organizational climate and morale as well as maintaining public support for their frequent and inevitably controversial actions. Despite some publicized behavior problems in the Mid-east conflicts, the professional and highly-trained military that the United States has developed since Vietnam provides reason to believe that prior initiatives to reduce or prevent inappropriate actions have met with at least some success, but that unrelenting vigilance may be a crucial prerequisite for continued improvement in preventing unacceptable behaviors in the American Military during wartime.

Finally, and commensurate with the substantive conclusions outlined above, this article demonstrates the conceptual efficacy of "organizational evil" for generating unconventional insights into the nature of war in general, and the Vietnam War in particular, as well as providing additional evidence of the continuing viability of Bryant's typology as a tool for furthering an understanding of crime and deviant behavior in the military context. In addition, events such as the Tiger Force Operations also provide support for Bryant's suggestion that even tacit acquiescence, much less active approval of functional deviance in military organizations can significantly inhibit the prevention of dark side activities, suggesting that preventing such socially and ethically unacceptable behaviors will be a continuing challenge.

WHERE DOES THAT LEAVE US? SOME FINAL THOUGHTS

While war may be unavoidable at times, armed conflict is arguably inherently evil, to include creating a compatible environment for deviance. It is clear that in war troops are trained in the skills of killing the enemy, skills which require strong leadership to focus and control those skills to maintain the important adherence to the "rules of war." That adherence is critical if a military force is to succeed in avoiding the slippery slope of both individual deviance, and especially the possibility of the emergence of organizational evil, especially in the face of the fact that military forces tend to demonize the enemy. Such demonization may well be effective in focusing troops on the mission of defeating an enemy, but that demonization may also lead to inappropriate deviance if not well controlled. To avoid the pitfalls of individual deviance or allowing organizations to take on an environment, the importance of strengthening value based ethics on the part of military forces to help guide appropriate

behavior cannot be overstated. In the final analysis it is effective and

ethical leadership that is critical to controlling and guiding individual

and organizational military actions along ethically normative paths.

REFERENCES

Allen, Joe, (2006). "Death Row at the Castle, the Mere Gook Rule," *International Socialist Review*, Issue 47, May-June 2006.

Allison, William T., (2007). "Military Justice in Vietnam: The Rule of Law in an American War," *Law and Politics Book Review*, Vol. 17, No. 5. pp 366-368. http://www.bsos.umd.edu/gvpt/lpbr/reviews/2007/05/military-justice-in-vietnam-rule-of-law.html, Accessed June 26, 2012.

Anonymous (1969). "The Massacre at Hue," *Time Magazine*, October 31, 1969.

Brush, Peter, (2010). "Fragging in Vietnam, " http://www.library.vanderbilt.edu/central/Brush/brush.htm#articles, accessed June 26, 2012.

Bryant, Clifton D. (1979). *Khaki-Collar Crime: Deviant Behavior in the Military Context.* New York: The Free Press.

Card, David, (2000). "Going to College to Avoid the Draft," Unpublished paper, University of California, Berkley.

"Cholon," Online World Visitors Guide, http://worldvisitguide.com/sale/MS05170.html, accessed March, 20, 2012.

"The Evolution of the All Volunteer Force, (2006)." *Rand Research in Brief*, http//www.rand.org/pubs/research_briefs/RB9195/index1.html, accessed June 26, 2012.

Frosh, Frank, (1970). "Body Count a Factor," *Lodi News Sentinel*, http://news.google.com/newspapers?nid=2245&dat=19700521&id=AOgzAAAAIBAJ&sjid=1jIHAAAAIBAJ&pg=7335,4650493, accessed June 26. 2012.

Gartner, Sigmund and Myers, Marissa E., (1995). "Body Counts and "Success" in the Vietnam and Korean wars," *The Journal of Interdisciplinary History*, Vol. 25, No. 3, pp. 377-395.

Greenhill, Kelly M., (2006). "Don't Dumb Down the Army," *New York Times*, February 17, 2006, http://belfercenter.ksg.harvard.edu/publication/1519/dont_dumb_down_the_army.html, accessed March 20, 2012.

Greenberg, I. M., (1969) "Project 100,000: The Training of Former Rejectees," *The Phi Delta Kappan*, Vol. 50. No. 10 (June 1969), pp. 570-574.

Hersh, Seymour M., (2004). "Torture at Abu Ghraib," *The New Yorker*, May 10, 2004.
Hinkley, David (2013). "CBS apologizes for 'Amazing Race' segment that used Hanoi memorial as prop: Memorial, which features a downed American aircraft, had been a spot to search for clues," New York Daily News, March 24, 2013 (http://www.nydailynews.com/entertainment/cbs-apologizes-amazing-race-segment-article-1.1298177, accessed March 26, 2013).

James, Michhael S., (2003). "Demonizing the Enemy a Hallmark of War," ABC News, http://abcnews.go.com/International/story?id=79071, accessed June 26, 2012.

Jenkins, Loren, (2005). "Saigon the Last Day," NPR April 29, 2005. http://npr.org/templates/story.php?storyId=4624718, accessed June 26, 2012.

Jurkiewicz, Carol L., ed., (2012). *The Foundations of Organizational Evil*, Armonk, NY: M.E. Sharpe.

Jurkiewicz, Carol and Grossman, Dave, (2012). "Evil at Work," in *The Foundations of Organizational Evil*, Armonk, NY: M.E. Sharpe.

Kaplan, Roger., (1987). "Army Unit Cohesion in Vietnam: A Bum Rap." *Parameters*, September 1987. pp. 58-67.

Meine, Manfred F. and Dunn, Thomas P. (2012). "Policing the Police, Using Ethics Education and Training to Combat 'Official Deviance'." *Journal of US-China Public Administration,* Vol. 9, No. 9 (September 2012).

Moore, Roger and Collins, June, (1971). *The Khaki Mafia.* New York: Crown Publishers.

Nelan, Bruce W., Angello, Bonnie, and Thompson, Mark, (1995). "Vietnam : Lessons from the Lost war," *Time Magazine*, April 24, 1995.

Nowinski, Joseph (2012). "Foreword," in *The Foundations of Organizational Evil*, Armonk, NY: M.E. Sharpe.

Powell, Colin, (2012). *It Worked for Me, In Life and Leadership.* New York, NY: Harper Collins.

Raimondo, Tony, (Undated). The Mỹ Lai Massacre: A Case Study, School of the Americas, Fort Benning, Georgia, http://www.fsa.ulaval.ca/personnel/vernag/EH/F/cause/lectures/my-lai.htm, accessed June 26, 2012.

Rummel, R.J., (1997). "Statistics of Vietnamese Democide Estimates, Calculations, and Sources" in *Statistics of Democide: Genocide and Mass Murder Since 1900*, Transaction Publishers, Rutgers University.

Rumsfeld, Donald (2011). "Rumsfeld's Rules." Informal document provided directly to first author by Rumsfeld, March 2011.

Salla, Michael and Weiss, Mitch, (2006). *The Tiger Force.* New York: Little Brown and Co.

Sitikoff, Harvard, (1999). "The Postwar Impact of Vietnam," in *The Oxford Companion to American Military History*. Ed. John Whiteclay Chambers II. New York: Oxford UP.

Stein, Jeff, (1992). *A Murder in Wartime*, New York: St. Martins Press.

Sullivan, Patricia, (2005). "Obituaries: General Commanded Troops in Vietnam," *The Washington Post*, July 19, 2005.

Turse, Nick (2013). *Kill Anything that Moves*. New York, Henry Holt and Company.

The Vietnam Veteran's Memorial, The Wall-USA, http://thewall-usa.com/summary.asp, accessed June 26, 2012.

Westheider, James E., (2007). *The Vietnam War*, Westport, CT: Greenwood Press.

"What is a Hollow Force," (2011). Chief of Staff of the Air Force Strategic Studies Group, May 18, 2011, http://www.af.mil/shared/media/document/AFD-120213-053.pdf, accessed June 27, 2012.

AUTHORS NOTES:

NOTE 1: In both Vietnam and Germany, the author witnessed racial demonstration by African American soldiers. In the latter case the author was even tasked to supervise the surreptitious photographing of protestors for possible later disciplinary action.

NOTE 2: As a supervisory special agent in the Army's Criminal Investigation Division many of the investigations the author conducted and supervised related to drug use and drug smuggling, with the number of investigations straining investigative resources. It was common for special agents to investigate so many cases during their one year tours as investigative offices of five or more agents would investigate in other parts of the World.

NOTE 3: As a supervisory special agent in the Army's Criminal Investigation Division the author accompanied the lead agent in the investigation to the Special Forces compound in Nha Trang, Vietnam for the purpose of apprehending the organizations legal counsel for involvement in the cover-up. Upon arrival at the compound the team was contacted by investigative headquarters to cease their actions since the investigation had been halted.

NOTE 4: As a supervisory special agent in the Army's Criminal Investigation Division the author was involved in a number of investigations involving deserters who had been provided false documents to enable them to travel throughout South Vietnam to exchange military payment certificates into US Dollars or dollar instruments for well to do Vietnamese and Chinese merchants for transfer to offshore banks. The going rate for the deserters' efforts was reported to be $100 for each $1000 so converted. Penetrating these underworld style enterprises resulted in a number of covert investigative operations to penetrate such criminal organizations.

NOTE 5: As a supervisory special agent in the Army's Criminal Investigation Division the author was involved in the apprehension of a Special Forces officer for illegal money conversion of $2500. The ensuing investigation was not yet complete when the author turned the investigation over to another agent in preparation for departure from Vietnam. Despite the incomplete status the investigation had already identified over $250,000 of illegal conversions and the purchase of seven Corvette automobiles which were picked up in the US by people purporting to be this officer.

NOTE 6: As an apprentice investigator in Augsburg, Germany in the early 1960's, the author became involved in the initial effort to

investigate what later became the Khaki Mafia, to include talking
with the officer who first brought the problem to light. The initial
investigation was covered up by senior officials in that area, but was
later reopened. It was "squashed" a second time, but was reopened
when the Army created an independent investigative organization.
That final investigation led to Congressional hearings and
disciplinary actions against at least one general officer and the first
Sergeant Major of the Army, but no prosecutions.

NOTE 7: By the late 1960's and early 1970's, "fraggings" had
become a significant problem. As a supervisory special agent in the
Army's Criminal Investigation Division, the author personally
investigated two murders, and several attempted murders during a
one year tour in Vietnam, and supervised several additional such
incidents. While the term "fraggings" evolved because of soldiers
rolling fragmentation hand grenades into their leader's tents or other
living quarters, even into latrines, the term was also applied to
murders of officers and non-commissioned officers through the use
of firearms.

NOTE 8: These situations were attempted murder cases investigated
by the author, and would have been part of the so called "fragging"
statistics had they been successful.

www.ingramcontent.com/pod-product-compliance
Lightning Source LLC
Chambersburg PA
CBHW070934290526
45795CB00003B/1019